PRAYERS
FOR

Worship

PRAYERS FOR Worship

E. LEE PHILLIPS

WORD BOOKS
PUBLISHER

ISBN 0–8499–0137–5
Library of Congress catalog card number: 78–65814
Printed in the United States of America

*For
Lynn,
my twin brother,
who keeps giving me
new meanings for courage*

Contents

Introduction

Prayer is, or ought to be, the language of sacrament, of mystery, of naming the Loving Stranger who meets us at the crossing of swollen streams, at the junctures of pain, distress, and joy in our lives.

Sometimes it is best expressed without any words, in the eloquence of yearning, the mime of the spirit, the silence of deep passion. All the great mystics have understood this. A sense of presence gathers like beads of nectar in the quietness of waiting, of simply being there and anticipating Him whose coming is like the dawn, transforming everything. The soul shivers in the night air, expecting it.

And even when prayer is spoken, especially as public utterance, it should be in words born out of the silence and the waiting, words pregnant with mystery, words opening into consciousness like blossoms bursting naturally in the springtime air. Anything less is a travesty, and prejudices the mind to believe that transactions of the spirit are far more shallow than they really are.

Lee Phillips understands this. His prayers are exceptional. They breathe an air of exquisite taste and gentle grace, like a room filled with fine china, old masters, and fresh bouquets of forget-me-nots.

Lee is clearly a poet, seized at once with what Meister Eckhardt called the *Istigkeit* of God—the divine *is*ness—and with the realities of life and environment as tangible expressions of that *is*ness. His images do not so much startle the mind as gently tempt it along the lines of thoughtfulness and revery, until suddenly it finds itself in the presence of the Transcendent One.

The presence, we know, has been there all along. It is the discovery itself that is startling.

I especially like what these prayers know of the human condition—the pain of loneliness, the beauty of age, the weight of grief, the delicate, almost withdrawn, flutterings of hope. They show the marks of listening—of being present to God until the world itself becomes transparent to Him, until the *facticities* of daily existence break through their barrier of commonness to ask a blessing.

God knows we need such prayers for our worship today. Public worship, at its best, is extended prayer, even in hymn and sermon, and the mood is kept most faithfully by the actual moments of voiced approach. Too often we have let it all down with slipshod preparation, either in ourselves or in the words of our petitions. But here are phrasings to teach us the rhythm again, to restore the mood and tempt us into Presence. We could do much worse than follow them.

The sensitive minister will carry them into the pulpit with him or her, gladly sharing them with the congregation. And the creative minister, catching the tune, will learn to sing his or her own songs to God in similar language, happy that the original singer was given to our age.

JOHN KILLINGER

The Importance of
Vital Public Prayer Today

A noted English clergyman visited this country some years ago. When his visit was concluded and he was preparing to return to England, he was asked what impressed him most about American worship. He replied, "The badness of your prayers."

Good public prayers are one of the great overlooked tasks in the worship life of the present day evangelical church. The worst that can happen to the prayer life of the church is to take it for granted; allow it to become rote, perfunctory, routine, stagnant; to dilute its potency through misuse and its power through neglect.

To slight public prayer is to be insensitive to the workings of the Holy Spirit. It is to stress minors and neglect the majors, to misconstrue and confuse priorities, to demean worship's joyous intent and didactic possibilities.

This facet of the church's life has been ignored long enough. Public prayer enlightens the way and helps mark the course the community of faith will follow. Redemption takes on reality in prayers and liturgies that aid in confession, receiving pardon, scriptural instruction, realigning personal and community priorities, and deepening personal piety. When this imperative task takes a back seat to lesser concerns, the tendency is toward neurotic expressions of faith—intellectual detachment or emotional overreactions. There is considerable evidence that this form of spiritual apathy and its resultant outcomes are rampant in many American Protestant churches today. There is a deep yearning among evangelical Christians for something more.

Witness the expectations often attendant to the pastoral prayer: The congregation gathers—waiting, expectant, hopeful. Now comes the moment like no other in the week when not only the Word will be read and explained, the best a struggling servant of God can explain it, but a prayer will be prayed—many prayers—and there rides on these corporate acts of worship, intertwined between music, liturgy, and the sacraments, the fondest hopes, deepest needs, and sacred longings of the people of God. They have been here before. Solace, comfort, inspiration, insight, justice, challenge—all these expressions of the grace of God have been known to them before and they expect them to happen again. They have been met before, they have been filled before, they have arrived with heart broken or spirit rejoicing and wondered silently, "Will the minister pray today about what I have been feeling, about my fears and burdens, about my desires and aspirations, about what really concerns me?" And when the gathered worship of the body of Christ is over, they exclaim in a way that reverberates in the soul, affirming an awareness of the presence of God almost beyond description, "The minister prayed from my corner. He knew where I stood; he saw not only the surface appearance but the problem beneath the surface, and he worded it with a vision and a vocabulary that put me in touch with God and met my need."

The minister who delivers an effective pastoral prayer has learned that outward expression reveals inward intention. Prayer reveals us. We learn to pray by praying. We become what we pray.

Whether a minister prays from a vital personal relationship with God and a sense of the presence of Christ that is undeniably real or prays hesitantly, routinely, out of a vacuum, can be instantly detected. It is a matter beyond vocabulary. It has to do with the temperature of the soul, something emanating from the heart. There is a difference between addressing God, a remote Being with whom one seldom converses, and communicating with the Father in whom one feels love and trust and guidance, because it is a part of a continuing, greatly treasured, and heartbeat close relationship. We pray no larger than our trust in God, no deeper than our walk with the Savior.

Prayer, asking and receiving, waiting silently or praying in unison, is communion with God. It is the heartbeat of the soul. Therefore every effort should be made to compose and shape worship prayers that are true to the ways of God and faithful to the needs of persons.

There is no substitute for solid study, creative brooding, and informed writing by the person who would pray well in public. This task calls for meditation, inspiration, a stillness of the heart, a receptivity of the mind, a garnering of quiet within the soul, an openness to the disciplines of the spiritual life.

Many nonliturgical Protestant denominations do not lay an appropriate emphasis nor provide proper theological training in their seminaries on the importance of substantive creative worship leadership. The "how" of formulating worship prayers is largely left to chance. The following examples demonstrate ways some ministers handle this responsibility.

A Minister without Time

Reverend Buford Johnson, though not a college graduate, has been pastor of the 150-member Third Street Church for twenty years. In that time he has ministered to two generations and has gathered quite a following. With the advancing years he has begun to project a grandfatherly image. Greatly loved by his people, the recent twentieth anniversary celebration of his pastorate was a milestone in his life.

Pastor Johnson has been very busy this week. On Monday and Tuesday he was out of town at a conference on "bus ministry." Wednesday, the funeral home called. Pastor Johnson's name is on file there as a minister who may be contacted in case a family in grief has no pastor. This will be his third funeral through this source in as many weeks. This most recent service is for a family that requested a minister though they do not attend church or believe in attending church. The financial remuneration from these pastoral functions is greatly appreciated by the minister's large family.

After the funeral Friday, he is going to work on his Sunday sermon. He liked the text chosen for the funeral, so he will expand on it for an hour Friday afternoon, and Saturday evening after the television movie is over he will put the finishing touches on the outline. Because his text is "In my Father's house are many mansions, if it were not so I would have told you," he has decided to preach on "Heavenly Housing."

The pastoral prayer Sunday will be the usual spontaneous response the congregation has come to expect. He will pray for the nation, "the leaders of our land," "the sick, the lonely, the tempted, the oppressed," referring to "each and every one" and "each and every need," requesting God "to warm our hearts, be with us through the rest of this service and we will be sure to give you all the praise. Amen."

Last Sunday, Pastor Johnson included four lines from "Take Time to Be Holy" in his pastoral prayer. He kept a hymnal open to the proper page so he could quote it at the appropriate moment.

He also included two other important interests. They just came to him and he had a feeling they were right. He prayed that the budget would be met that Sunday and that their present building campaign would be "to the glory of God and the advancement of the kingdom." He did not mention these money matters in his lengthy announcements since he liked to take that time to make the visitors really feel welcome, but he felt the congregation got the point.

He also felt inspired to pray for aging Mrs. Kimberly, who was living in a nursing home. She had taught the older ladies Sunday School class for thirty years and was one of the best loved members of the church. Her finances were nearly depleted. The church had been assisting her; many persons felt sorry for her. At eighty-six, she was deaf and almost blind. The pastor felt inspired to pray for her, so singling out only this one person, he closed his prayer, mentioning her needs.

A Minister Who Takes Time

Dr. George Edward Fitzpatrick at Westminster, has spent three mornings this week on his Sunday worship. The sermon text and title had been chosen in the summer at his Canadian retreat. Planning with reference to a lectionary and in light of national religious and local observances, he had mapped out a yearly program of preaching.

In correlation with his minister of music and minister of education, the order of worship was composed on Monday. A duet with guitar and clarinet was planned as the prelude. The minister of education had a brief call to worship of four lines. The pastor had written a one-paragraph confession of sin based on sins of attitude, pride, and lethargy. A litany of praise, written by members of the fifth and sixth grades of the church school had been ready for use for three weeks. The pastor and worship committee tried to include as much of the church family as possible in planning and executing worship.

When the order of worship was typed up by the pastor's secretary prior to being printed, the pastor sat down and sought to correlate his pastoral prayer with all aspects of the service. Paying particular attention to the Scripture reading and text, he often would include a line or portion of a line from the text in his pastoral prayer. This provided continuity with the sermon and enabled a major theme to emerge.

Dr. Fitzpatrick was a middle-aged man who had served on the mission field for ten years. When he returned to the states because of his wife's health, Westminster felt his gifts as president of a Presbyterian seminary in Asia, where he taught practical theology in the fields of preaching and pastoral care, would give them a strength and solidness needed to aid in the cohesion of their large, diverse, inner-city congregation.

In his five years at Westminster, Dr. Fitzpatrick had proven to be prayer-oriented and very sensitive to the fundamental pressing needs of the people. He was a man of insight and wisdom, who took time for private meditation. He gave a mystical expression to public prayer that was rare.

Dr. Fitzpatrick remembers the needs of his parishioners by visualizing them in his mind as they might sit in their pews on Sunday morning. In that frame of mind he walks the aisles of the church and recalls: ethical temptations that face two business partners; several marriages with problems of communication and trust; college students returning for the holidays and the identity struggle many of them face; an elderly couple, the husband recovering from a heart attack and the wife facing major surgery next week; a physician pondering some form of medical mission service as an expression of his faith; a childless couple who want to adopt; a recent widow who lost her husband two weeks ago, now suffering the full brunt of loneliness; the hospitalized mother of a large family who lingers near death, kept alive by life-sustaining machines, a situation rapidly draining the family finances; and some of the poignant confessions shared in the weekly Alcoholics Anonymous meeting held at the church Thursday evening.

Westminster worship addresses the contemporary mind with dignity, sensitivity, and substance. The pastor, convinced the worship hour is pivotal, places great emphasis on content and spontaneity born of preparation. Dr. Fitzpatrick says the total worship event can be a life-changing, life-reorienting experience, and Westminster in joyful realization has come to feel the same way.

A Minister Attuned to the Times

Ms. Virginia Sparks was preparing her daughter for bed Tuesday night when a thought crossed her mind about a liturgy the pastor had asked her to compose for the worship service next Sunday. Although she had been associate pastor at Covenant Community Church for only two months, she felt some headway had been made in changing sexist attitudes in the worship of the church. Just last week she had talked with the pastor about his mostly exclusive male terminology for God. He had preached on the text "If any man is in Christ Jesus, he is a new creature." She indicated that although "man" was meant to include all the human family, she still felt left out. It was her opinion that his handling of the text left the impression that only males could be saved. At times there was a subtle implication, and at other times a not so subtle implication, that women were second-class persons not as important to God as men.

Ms. Sparks sought to be constructive in presenting awareness of sexist language. When references were made to man she often substituted the word *human* or *person*. Rather than using the pronoun *He* in saying that God caused or did something, she would use another name for God: "Creator," "the Almighty," or "Lord." She did not stress "Father" or "Heavenly Father." In her own liturgies and prayers she had occasionally referred to God as "Parent" and once as "Our Father-Mother." This brought a divided response from the congregation. Younger members, especially women, were delighted. Many older persons were upset with her—many more than cared to say anything to her. She did get a few hot phone calls, and the pastor received even more. She knew her presence threatened many Christians, yet she was never rude or defensive so as to deliberately alienate others. For the most part, experience had aided her in handling her own feelings and the extreme responses from others.

She was fortunate that the pastor and church board were open persons who welcomed her ministry and the life style it represented. The pastor had made every effort to change his stereotyped pattern of thinking, and she was impressed by his confession that he was not even aware of sexist comments or bias. It was a familiar confession and one she knew required her patience and understanding.

As the quiet of the evening fell around her and the stillness of her home surrounded her, she sat down at her desk and began to write:

"Daughters and Sons of God,
Descendants of Eve and Adam, Sarah and Abraham,
Rachel and Jacob, Ruth and Boaz,
Mary and Joseph,
Let us celebrate our lineage in the faith."

A Time That Shapes the Minister

Dr. Livingston Sanders, rector of Christ Episcopal Church, has given fifteen hours this week to his Sunday sermon. The lectionary has aided him in Scripture selection as he follows the traditional seasons of the church year. He does not worry about his worship prayers. His collects are chosen, uniform, impeccable in thought, tone, and language. He has only to repeat them with sincerity, something he does very well, and a large part of the verbal portion of his worship service is already guaranteed. The longer he lives the more grateful he becomes for *The Book of Common Prayer*.

On Saturday afternoon before dinner, Dr. Sanders had driven down to the church to find a telephone number he had apparently misplaced on Friday. He could not find the number at home and he was to call the family involved that evening.

On the way from his church study, he went into the sanctuary to pause for a moment at the altar. The ladies of the altar society had just finished their work an hour or so earlier. Crosses and candles, fresh flowers and altar cloths were all in place. The rector became very sensitive to the beauty of the moment: sunset beams through stained glass on an intricately carved, perfectly appointed altar.

There were moments when he was amazed at the events of his life the past two years. Following his seminary graduation, he had become the pastor of a small, Protestant, nonliturgical church in a rural area. The church members were warm and caring, life was unhurried and worship was simple. Much of what he had learned in seminary did not apply in his rural situation. After a few months of soul-searching and intensive inquiry shared with other ministers in various cities, he discovered his taste in worship was decidedly more formal than in his denomination. He entertained growing concern about the language used in prayer, the centrality of the Lord's Supper, and the need for closer ecumenical cooperation among churches. After lengthy discussions with his own church and denominational leaders, he resigned his country pastorate.

The next summer he found a church in which he felt a kinship and fealty of spirit. It was an Episcopal church, and one of its greatest appeals for him was the sense of formality and dignity in the prayer book. When he first read it, he was overwhelmed. He remarked that for months it was the sort of key he had been searching for. He felt found.

With Bishop Rutherford's wise counsel, plans were made for a year's additional study at the Episcopal Theological Seminary in Virginia. That year was culminated in his acceptance into the Episcopal ministry and his eventual appointment as rector at Christ's Church, a city parish.

A multitude of thoughts flooded his mind as he stood alone in meditation that moving Saturday afternoon. Quietly he knelt to pray. Softly he began to quote some of the collects of praise he had grown to love so well and had joyously committed to memory.

A Shared Time of Preparation

As the congregation of Lincoln Park Baptist looked over their order of worship they noted their call to worship was a brief responsive reading. The pastor said a line, then the congregation; six responses in all. They had grown fond of this approach and other similar innovations in their worship.

When they were considering a pastor, one of the things the pulpit committee found most attractive about Dr. Maxwell was his knowledge of creative worship. He seemed to know what he was doing and he appeared to know how to involve them. In the two years since he had become their pastor, this proved to be the case and they loved it. Never had so much freshness and vitality reigned in their worship.

In other years the order of worship was condensed into single lines on one page. Now their order of worship was three and a half pages in an attractive bulletin. On the cover was a small corner drawing of the church steeple, the rest of the page was given to an arresting, informative quote from a churchman or from a relevant book. Inside, plenty of room was provided for congregational responses. Dr. Maxwell led the church in their first unison calls to worship, litanies of faith, and benedictions. Each Sunday these responses varied. They were brief, tasteful, thoughtful, and inspiring. Very little objection had been raised because this procedure seemed to make good sense: it deepened them spiritually, it involved them mentally, it added the freshness of new dimensions in prayer.

Dr. Maxwell had a noteworthy way of correlating his worship services. He maintained an active worship committee where members rotated every eight weeks. He was a believer in staff meetings. Each minister shared in the formation of the order of worship. The music ministry balanced the prayers, the prayers correlated with the sermon, the total service had a symmetry and progression that was well timed and appropriate. If the sermon, a focal point of worship, was on missions or faith, then all other aspects of the service correlated with that theme: Scripture readings, pastoral prayer, and anthems.

The worship services at Lincoln Park have a timely progression and direction. Opening prayers and calls to worship stress quietness and receptivity, enabling the worshiper to withdraw from the world and seek fellowship with the Spirit of God. All responsive parts of the worship are brief, with an emphasis on simple words and statements of faith. They have a flow and a poetic brevity that is easy to read and comprehend. Hymns and Scripture readings lead toward new vistas in the worship service. The pastoral prayer plunges the depths of personal concern, confession of sin, gratitude, and petition, with specificity. In that moment, when Dr. Maxwell seeks to state publicly the deep concerns of the people, the combined prayers of Christians for themselves and one another becomes a holy moment, alive with quiet supplications and the deep longings of a people of faith.

Invitations seem a prayer in themselves. Unpretentious, without manipulation or overlaid with guilt, they follow the arresting and challenging truths of the sermon in a bidding infused with love. The benedictions, a special concern of the pastor, seem to convey that "there is one more thing I want to say." They are short and direct, like the comments of some persons to friends or family: "Remember, we love you," or, "Our prayers go with you." The benedictions remind the worshiper of what has taken place and send him on his way with a final blessing: a word of Presence in adversity, peace in the storm, joy in struggle, or hope in sorrow; all through faith in the Son of God.

A new spirit of joyousness and celebration has manifested itself at suburban Lincoln Park Church. Worship is planned, but with room for flexibility, freedom, and originality. The use of many musical instruments, graded choirs, ballet, media presentations, Scripture readings by families, variety in the observance of the Lord's Supper has caused fresh breezes to move the church into new and exciting ways of presenting the gospel and representing Christ to a needy world.

Lately, many have been asking, What is this new spirit we hear about at Lincoln Park Church? Most of those who come to find out, come back to celebrate, to pray and to serve, to listen for God who moves in mysterious, often exciting ways "His wonders to perform."

Good public prayers are a matter of heart and mind. The psalmist prayed that the words of his mouth and the meditations of his heart would be acceptable in the sight of the Lord. We pray to a God of holiness, mystery, justice, and love. God is our Creator. All that we are and have we owe to the Lord. Respect, humility, and praise must characterize the speech of prayer. This requires all the intelligence and compassion a person possesses. It means hard work. If we are to love God with all our mind, it means digging. It means avoiding imitation like the plague; caring enough about the spiritual struggle of others to find and give our creative best.

There is no legitimate call for public prayer to lose its dignity and beauty in an effort to be modern. Prayer that places God in an overly familiar position, as though addressing another buddy, and includes slang, as it plays havoc with respectable English, conveys a distorted view of God. It embraces cheap language as adequate for Kingly intercourse, and reflects more on passing fads and changing milieus than on the rightful honor appropriate in addressing the Lord of the Universe.

To show a sense of awe and respect in the presence of the Almighty and to communicate a conception of the cross-laden, resurrection-real, and personally abiding love of God lays an enormous burden on those who pray in public, be they pastors or lay persons. Liturgy in our day is being seen as something that emanates from the needs of the people. It exists for them; it is the expression of biblical truths for their edification. Indeed, the prayers of verbal and unison response are to be the work of all those who love God, bound in the community of faith for worship and service. Pastors are forming worship committees to share in this task; the priesthood of all believers is being encouraged. In the church each of us has a ministry to perform, and the contributions of the saints are needed in corporate worship to give expression to the uniqueness of the local body of Christ and to establish its identity. Pastors are learning the joy of being enablers, coaches, standing in the background and aiding others in achieving the potential of their gifts.

The principles, then, that apply to the pastor's preparation in prayer, carry the same weight with other members of the church who join in composing the litanies, liturgies, and confessions: not only must they be acquainted with the Bible and a theological framework, but they must do their homework with dictionary and grammar as well. The fluent preparer of worship prayers must wrestle with syntax and phraseology to extract the choicest words and craft the most lucid lines. The pastor, by virtue of his advanced educational studies and continual application of them, should be a wordsmith, winnowing from the dictionary the choicest vocabulary to merge the mutual concerns of persons into public utterances of appropriate prayer.

Great language is not the use of unusual words in an unusual way; it is the use of common words in an uncommon way. Placing them in a fresh, balanced new manner, deft, succinct, and vivid, can bring added impact and insight to their content. Poets can give us many a clue. They can teach us to cherish the lean, strong line, devoid of adjectives, adverbs, and clauses better left unsaid. We know the Twenty-Third Psalm, the Lord's Prayer, and the Gettysburg Address; we know better than we do.

The choicest collects, prayers, and liturgies of the ages become background for forging a style of one's own. Originality demands personal integrity, and diligent, honest work. So, we must toil, never to parrot another's style but to forge one of our own, remembering that our honest, sought-for word, is every bit as worthy as that of a pulpit master, much-admired. One must pray, producing the singular sound such a master found in the celebration and the love of God.

The speed at which the world is moving forces us to come to terms with the rapidly changing vocabulary of the times. Sophisticated technology, communication, travel have all contributed to this great flux. New terms emerge overnight, and publishers of dictionaries rush to release "new" and "updated" versions. The effect on the church has been monumental. New translations of Scripture have come in a deluge. Most major denominations have made revisions of their hymnals and liturgies in an effort to keep pace with the musical upheavals and vocabulary of our day. Some of them, five years later, are dated.

There is a healthiness, a vigor and foresight on the part of the churches who become convinced that this is the wrong time in the history of the world and the history of the church to ignore the winds of change. To lean lackadaisically on the tried and true of forms ignores their intent to be fluid, shaped, altered, and enriched according to the demands of the day.

It has perhaps never been so difficult to be true to the language of the day and yet classic in our verbal expressions. The freedom of change can work both ways—toward the transitory or toward the search for the lasting. This paradox complicates the task, yet makes it more challenging.

There is a fine line between the appropriate and the inappropriate word and every minister must find his peace and place in this task. We must avoid novelty for the sake of novelty, but at the same time experiment with taste and discretion to infuse new life into old forms and incorporate new cadences into the steps of a new age. This calls for discernment, for educated and courageous insight, so that we may stand in the midst of the tension and utter the prayerful word that is needed.

If fulfilling that need is to happen, then something beyond words will happen also. The minister, for instance, prepares a pastoral prayer for the appointed hour of worship, but the pastoral prayer also prepares the minister. Becoming ready, alert, sensitized to the Spirit of God is not totally word preparation, it is person preparation. Now, mind and heart merge together with other possibilities and ramifications.

When the minister prays in public and the local body of Christ is at prayer, he is not addressing the people on behalf of God, as in a sermon; he is addressing God on behalf of the people. The emphasis should not be on the minister but on the Lord to whom he intercedes. The minister, under the guidance of the Holy Spirit, should seek to move the attention of those present toward God. In prayer the Presence of God impregnates silence and fills the verbal and the nonverbal with that reality beyond the reach of vocabulary and the analysis of reason. The Presence, transcendent, infinite, and holy, is clothed in mystery, yet real as the faith that binds us in love through our Lord, Jesus Christ. We have met in His name and there, in our midst, is God, just as He promised!

We are being changed now, shaped, altered, molded from within. The grace of God takes us where we are, to where we never dreamed we would be, if we trust, and in that trust love Him whom we do not fully comprehend but whom we grasp well enough to desire forever.

"Be still and know that I am God" is not only the attitude prerequisite to prayer, it is the way to worship that issues into strength for life. In prayer's quiet communion Christ meets us. And the meeting is what matters!

PRAYERS
FOR
Worship

CALLS TO WORSHIP

1

Minister. What motivates your worship?
People. What we know of God in the past
Leads us to trust God in the present
And follow Him in the future.
Minister. Your faith is deeply rooted.
What of the unexplained?
People. We have much work to do,
Yet what we have seen
And experienced of God
Leads us to trust Him
For what we do not see
And do not understand.
Minister. With such expectations,
Faith blossoms,
Hope is born anew,
And the love of God is made real
Through Christ our Lord.

2

Minister. We have come to worship God.
　　　　　What are your concerns?
People.　　To learn of God.
Minister. By the statutes of God we are taught.
People.　　To be shaped by the wisdom of God.
Minister. By the precepts of God we learn to live.
People.　　To experience the guidance of God.
Minister. By the Holy Spirit we are led.
People.　　To be redeemed.
Minister. By grace through faith we are saved.
People.　　To be kept in the love of God.
Minister. Jesus said, "All the time I will be with
　　　　　you, to the very end of the world."
All.　　　　We praise the Lord, the God of our salva-
　　　　　tion.
　　　　　We worship Him in Spirit and in truth.
　　　　　Amen.

3

Minister. Who comes to worship God?
People.　　Husbands and wives,
　　　　　Brothers and sisters,
　　　　　Widows and widowers, we come.
Minister. The Lord is merciful toward all.
　　　　　God is no respecter of persons.

People. The rich and the poor,
The young and the old,
The sick and the well, we come.

Minister. The Lord searches for the lost,
For all salvation became flesh in Christ Jesus.

People. The proud and the lonely,
The alienated and the accepted,
The members and the seekers, we come.

Minister. This is a community of faith, of acceptance and reconciliation. Be ye reconciled to God and one another.

All. Just as we are we come to Thee,
O God of our salvation.

4

Minister. God's mighty acts among us are well known.

People. We are a people of history.

Minister. God's redemptive acts were epitomized in Christ Jesus.

People. We are a people of faith.

Minister. God's salvation gives us hope and courage to affect history.

People. We are a people of vision.

Minister. God cherishes fellowship with us in worship.

People. We are a people of prayer and praise.

All.   We are ready to magnify the Lord.
May our lives magnify
What we have been given,
What we are,
And what, by God's grace,
We may become. Amen.

5

Minister. Welcome to the house of the Lord,
Why have you come?
People.   We are here to worship God;
to see visions with the foresight of
youth,
to dream dreams with the wisdom of
age,
to move mountains with the power of
faith.
Minister. You are a daring people,
What gives you this boldness?
People.   The victory of our Lord Jesus Christ
over sin and death,
The promise of His life in us.
Minister. As is your faith, so be it unto you, and
more.
All.   That is our prayer also. Amen.

6

Minister. Trust the Lord.
People. Faith can lead to strength.
Minister. Honor the Lord.
People. Obedience can lead to wisdom.
Minister. Serve the Lord.
People. Duty can lead to fulfillment.
Minister. Praise the Lord.
People. Worship can lead to a joyful heart.
All. Lord, lead our worship to maturity
and our faith to fruition,
in the strength of this hour. Amen.

7

Minister. What happens in this hour matters to God and may be life-changing for you. Do you see the possibilities?
People. We may be brought up short, due to our sins.
We may be convicted of good deeds left undone.
We may discover hurts we inflicted, unaware of our intent.
Minister. Yes, mistakes may be made clearer.
People. We may also learn more of grace,
Hope may meet us in our despair,

Love may guide us to new vistas in faith.

Minister. Yes, the ways of holiness challenge the human spirit.

All. Praise to God, who accepts us in our error
And loves us to a richer life. Amen.

8

Minister. Glory to the Lord,
People. For He has dominion over all the earth.
Minister. Serve the Lord,
People. So all peoples and nations may praise Him.
Minister. Worship the Lord,
People. That we may be made perfect in His will.
All. Call forth from us, Lord, wise response.
Lead us to intelligent faith
And save us for Thy service. Amen.

9

Minister. What is special about this gathering?
People. It is not to magnify us
But to magnify the Lord.
Minister. How can this be?
People. We are God's creatures.

We serve the living Lord.
We are Christ's royal priesthood.
Minister. What is your intention?
People. Not only to magnify God in this place
but in our homes and our country
And to spread God's love to all persons.
Minister. How will this be accomplished?
All. Giving our money generously,
Visiting the unloved and lonely,
Examining our hearts closely
And praying diligently.
This is our worship, this is our praise.

10

Minister. Holy, Holy, Holy, Lord God of Hosts.
People. The whole earth is filled with Thy goodness.
Minister. If we descend into the depths of the sea
or climb the highest mountain,
People. The Lord is there.
Minister. When we gather in the Name of the Lord, He has promised
People. To be in our midst.
Minister. The Lord of Hosts is in our presence.
All. We will seek the Lord while he may be found.
We will call upon Him while He is near.
We will forsake any wicked way
And return unto our God. Amen.

11

Minister. Worship God,
People. Who of old is the same and forever true.
Minister. Praise God,
People. Who shows Himself anew and always
           with justice.
Minister. Magnify God,
All. He alone is worthy of our souls' delight
           and our lives' allegiance.

12

Minister. God is a God of mystery.
People. The holiness of God is His own.
Minister. God is a God of truth.
People. The wisdom of God is perfect.
Minister. God is a God of judgment.
People. The justice of God is without error.
Minister. God is a God of caring.
People. The love of God draws us through Christ
           Jesus into intimate fellowship with
           Him.
Minister. God, all Holy and all wise,
People. Receive our worship,
           The humble expression of our hearts'
             desire,

The joyous affirmation of our life in
Thee.
Amen.

13

Minister. Worship the Lord in holiness.
People. Honor is due the Name of our God.
Minister. Let all barriers be removed,
People. And all resistance done away.
Minister. Return unto the Lord in openness,
People. For God discloses Himself to the humble
And to the contrite He shows mercy.
Minister. Praise Him and extol His love,
People. For we are His people,
The objects of God's grace,
The recipients of God's love,
The crowning joy of God's
Creation.
The Lord be praised.

14

Minister. Welcome to this joyous celebration of life
in Christ Jesus.
People. Gladly do we come and gladly do we
acknowledge the Lordship of Christ.

Minister. Seek with your eyes to find truth.
Ask with your mind to probe alternatives,
Knock with your hands on the doors of
    need.
In so doing worship will inform living
And living will honor God.

All. We want to honor God with our lives
And we will begin in this glad hour of
    worship.

15

Minister. The rush of the world is with us.
People. Time borders us in every minute.
Minister. Anxiety creeps into our best hours.
People. Soon we are overborne with care.
Minister. How, then, shall we approach our wor-
    ship today?
People. We will cease activity and court receptiv-
    ity,
We will begin quietly,
    pray silently,
        and receive openly.
Minister. Such stillness is near to the heart of God;
Such discipline revives the Spirit.
Come each of you and open yourselves
    to the majesty of God.
People. We open ourselves. Come, Holy Spirit.
Amen.

PRAYERS FOR *Worship*

OPENING PRAYERS

1

Do something mighty in us today, Lord.

We grow complacent and reticent.
We are prone to become overly familiar
With holy things,
Leaving behind awe and reverence
And the majesty due thy Name.
Hide great hopes in our souls,
Stir mighty visions in our minds,
Fan noble desires in our hearts;
That more perfectly we may worship Thee,
More committedly we may serve Thee,
And more receptively we may be filled by Thee.

Do something mighty in us today, Lord.
Do Thou do it
For Thy Name's sake. Amen.

2

Our Father in heaven,
So often we find joy missing in our worship.
The predictability of the routine
Often dulls our capacity
For the unexpected, the exuberant,
And the excitement of spontaneity
In the gift of the moment.

Fill our worship
With fresh breezes of creativity.
Allow us to see with new vision
The variety of possibilities in prayer and praise.
Then bring us in delight
As real as grace
To celebrate Thy Holy Name. Amen.

3

When we pray to center ourselves
On the essentials of the faith, O Lord,
We often come up short,
Our spirits flagging,
Our trust waning,
Our lives out of focus.
We admit bringing to worship today
Hesitations, reluctance and doubt.

Enter our reticence with conquering love;
Expose us to the light of truth.
Draw us out, slow us down,
Forgive our sins, restore our vision.
Send us away with new resolve
Born of costly grace through The Suffering
    Servant. Amen.

4

From the restless movement and quickened pace
Of our everyday lives
We draw aside to catch the rhythms of Thy peace.

As the still small sounds of worship
Fill the high rooms of our souls
Breaking gradually into rainbow-colored
Choruses of praise,
Shape and mold us into godly men and women
Through Thy revelation in Christ Jesus. Amen.

5

A Vesper Prayer

Hushed is the world from toiling,

Quiet from fret and care.
Evening has spread its shadows
In sunset and twilight air.

Now in this hour abiding
Here let Thy love reside.
Lord, with Thy peace abounding
Draw us close to Thy side. Amen.

6

The rush of life is with us,
Contemplation nearly dies.
The din of noise confronts us,
Meditation passes by.
The ache of sorrow meets us,
Consolation finds us not.
Temptation tries our spirits,
Courage wanders from the fight.

Then we come to worship
To take hope in what is said,
To pause in quiet reverence
And be led to living bread.
Stir us, Lord, to praise Thee
In joyous song and quiet prayer.
Reacquaint us with Thy presence
And enfold us in Thy care. Amen.

7

There is no tongue can utter all
Our joy and celebration.
There are no words to state in full
Our love and adoration.
Therefore in prayer's soft silent sphere
Where men seem mute but God can hear,
Our lives attuned with grateful praise
Worship Thee, Lord, in all our ways. Amen.

8

Lord, our God,
Expand our horizons with visions of need.
Stir us with reality so vivid
That we cannot remain content with complacence
Nor comfortable with neglect.

Grant us the spiritual fortitude
That takes Love as its companion
And marches straightforwardly
Into the broken bones
And festering sores of our world,
Wherever they are found.

Let us spend ourselves unreservedly
In Thy service,

Through worship that orients
And deeds that save.
Through Christ, our Redeemer. Amen.

9

Lord, it is from a world divided against itself
That we merge into this hallowed place today
To worship Thee.
We too would be healers, reconcilers, redeemers,
As was Thy Son, Jesus.
Help us to catch the light of that calling
And spread it wherever we go,
Because of Thy love for us
And our love for Thee. Amen.

10

God of our worship, Lord of our lives,
Grant such a receptivity of mind
And ordering of affections
That petty cares offered to Thee
Would recede before the vision of Thy holiness
To be viewed again against the backdrop
Of the impoverished and hungry.

Let not our comforts lull us into lethargy
Nor our privileges into blindness.
Reorient and realign all in us
That passes by the person in need.
Make us sensitive to our opportunities.
This is our prayer
Because Thy will is the desire of our souls
And the supreme goal of our lives. Amen.

11

Surprise us, Father,
With open grace
And generous mercy
For depleted spirits
And troubled minds.

Inspire us, Father,
With fresh insight
And new vision
For divided loyalty
And waning trust.

Fill us, Father,
With moral courage
And needed strength
For sound thought
And godly living. Amen.

12

Lord,
As the loud voices
Of a competing world
Vie for our attention,
Allow us to embrace the silence
Of communion with Thee
That calms our troubled minds
And restores our inner lives.

Still us within,
Surround us without,
Guide us from above
Till in Thy calmness
We are readied in prayer
For worship and praise. Amen.

13

Lord, our God,
Bid us acknowledge Thee this hour,
Aware that our minds may be illumined,
Our emotions stirred,
Our motives rearranged,
When in the precincts of prayer
We call Thy Name
And seek Thy face.

Lord, our Maker,
Bid us adore Thee this hour,
Aware that our souls may be enlightened,
Our wills addressed,
Our attitudes challenged,
When in the act of praise
We call Thy Name
And seek Thy face.

Lord, our Redeemer,
Bid us magnify Thee this hour,
Aware that our thoughts may be disturbed,
Our preconceptions examined,
Our suppositions questioned,
When in the depths of contemplation
We call Thy Name
And seek Thy face. Amen.

14

Lord, honor our prayer of openness.
In seeking we are expectant.
In knocking we are hopeful.
In asking we are readied
By Thy Spirit,
For Thy leading,
In Thy Name. Amen.

15

An Evening Prayer

As evening stretches shadows
On the length of setting sun,
And the peace of quiet vespers
Unravels care as day is done,
Let us bring to God our burdens,
Our failures, hopes and prayers,
And let the gathering darkness
Gather us in God's dear care. Amen.

PRAYERS
FOR
Worship

PRAYERS OF
CONFESSION

1

Lord, when we could have done better
We preferred the easy way out.
We confess our guilt:
For building virtues from our vices
   instead of insight from our suffering;
For passing by the confined
   instead of sharing time with them;
For preferring the bright lights of the debasing
   instead of the Light of the world;
For acknowledging the thin layers of affluence
   and ignoring the poverty beneath;
For destroying good reputations by malicious words
   and believing it will not return double;
For loving ourselves haphazardly
   and imagining it would not affect
   all our relationships.

Please forgive us; reverse our priorities and
Renew our minds after the mind of Christ,
Through whom we pray. Amen.

2

Merciful God,
Nearer than we know
And closer than we feel,
Break down all wrong desire,
Smite every stumbling passion,
Remove any greedy pride
That stands between us and Thee.
We are prone to denial,
Given to procrastination,
And fond of excuses.
We make haste to blame others,
Protest our innocence,
And, only as a last resort, repent.
Forgive our stubbornness.
We project on others our weaknesses.
Greet our penitence with divine pardon
And our new resolve with understanding mercy,
Through Christ our Lord. Amen.

3

Forgive us, O Lord,
For lives unadjusted to the order of Thy love
And the familiarity of Thy counsel.
Forgive us also:
For living too seldom cognizant of Thy Word;

For hearts too seldom in rhythm with Thy
  compassion;
For hands too seldom content with their portion;
For ambitions too seldom in line with Thy Will;
For attitudes too seldom shaped by Thy love;
For morals so seldom obedient to Thy law;
For tongues so seldom accustomed to confession.

O Thou who freest us in pardon
And givest us a new chance,
Cleanse us, we pray, and align us again
With the familiarity of Thy instruction.
Through Jesus Christ our Lord. Amen.

4

We are sorry, God, for our wayward handling of
  life.
We have squandered time, hoarded money, avoided
  challenges, and used others.
We have borne waiting grievously, illness
  stubbornly, trials reluctantly, and responsibility
  half-heartedly.
We have doubted Thy care, mistrusted Thy
  providence, distorted Thy power, and ignored
  Thy love.
We have neglected our discipleship, injured our
  relationships, sabotaged our fellowship, and
  underrated Thy forgiveness.

Forgive us now, we pray,
And let us try again,
Sensitive to Thy Spirit
And committed to Thy Will. Amen.

5

All.   Forgive us, O Lord, our transgressions:
Minister. For running ahead
People.   And trailing behind;
Minister. For squandering money
People.   And abusing time;
Minister. For manipulating others
People.   And avoiding ourselves;
Minister. For avowing mercy
People.   And practicing prejudice;
Minister. For desiring peace
People.   And promoting war;
Minister. For keeping the law
People.   And distorting its spirit;
Minister. For limiting alternatives
People.   And prejudging results;
Minister. For raising questions
People.   And ignoring the answers;
Minister. For worshiping failures
People.   And forgetting forgiveness.
All.   From these devious sins
            And repeated errors
            We now repent. Amen.

6

Lord, do not let us do more
If in doing less we might do it better.
Do not let us acquire more
If in living with less
We might know Thee better.
We are easily swayed by size,
Equating quantity with quality,
Wealth with security,
And applause with popularity.
Forgive us for spreading ourselves thin
For the sake of appearances.
Permit us to amend our ways
Lest we miss the Baby in the stable,
The Lad in the carpenter's shop,
The Teacher on the hillside,
And the Christ on the Cross. Amen.

7

Forgive us, Almighty God,
For camping on the periphery
And living on the border,
Never facing the central sins of our lives.

Made for Thy truth,
We are deceptive and untruthful.

Blessed with intelligence,
We seek Thy wisdom sporadically.
Capable of deep caring,
We want to be congratulated and cared for.
Created for fellowship,
We are too busy to pray.
Endowed with plenty,
We hoard the best part.
Intended for the deep,
We court the trivial.

These circles of folly
Surround our sin of rebellion against Thee;
What we were made to enjoy in abundance
We reject with pride.
Pardon us, we pray.
Sin confessed looses its grip on us.
Therefore strengthen us in Thy mighty hand
And center us through faith in Jesus Christ, our
Lord. Amen.

8

People.   Lord, Thy watchcare over us is
unending.
Though we forget Thee
Thou hast not forgotten us.
Though we deny Thee
Thou hast not denied us.
Though we do not understand Thee

Thou hast not misunderstood us.
Though we ignore Thee
Thou hast not ignored us.
Minister. This is the root of our transgression:
While expecting God to live up
To what we want for ourselves,
We have not lived up to what we know of
    God.
Our pride has blinded us.
All. Lord, forgive our sins of presumption and
    pompousness.
Refashion our expectations after Thy
    Will
And our trust after Thy love. Amen.

9

God of our salvation,
We confess these sins too long kept private,
Blinding our vision of Thee:
Laziness that called the hours useless;
Indifference that treated need as untouchable;
Pride that considered self superior to God;
Hate that disfigured us and damaged others;
Greed that denied our lot and coveted more;
Compromise that diluted our convictions;
Gluttony that treated world hunger with disdain;
Prejudice that treated the disturbed as unclean;
Stubbornness that denied apology its chance.

Pardon our failures, lest they go on unchecked
And we go on far from Thee.
Keep us in Thy fold,
Through our Savior, Christ the Lord. Amen.

10

Lord, giver of life,
Through our relationship in Christ Jesus
We have been offered many good gifts:
Freedom is ours but we want no restrictions;
Hope is ours but we want a guarantee.
Joy is ours but we want it immediately.
Peace is ours but we want to hoard it.
Love is ours, but we can't believe it.

Forgive us for placing our wants above Thy grace,
For limiting Thy goodness by our selfishness,
For expecting quick answers to eternal verities.
In the Name of Jesus, we pray. Amen.

11

Gracious heavenly Father,
Who art more to us than all else in life
And who standest beside us when all else fails;

Forgive us for emotions that betray
A lack of trust in Thee.

We become impatient,
Preventing time from teaching us.
We become anxious,
Stifling faith from strengthening us.
We become insensitive,
Impeding love from deepening us.

We tend to equate human nature
With divine will and to depend on
Religious rituals for saving faith.

These attitudes have separated us from Thee.
We do not want to live this way again.
Restore us to right relationship with Thee
And lead us to trust again,
Through Christ our Lord. Amen.

12

Hold our requests in abeyance, Lord,
Until we are willing to serve instead of be served;
Until we are more concerned for justice than our
    comfort;
Until we walk the second mile without complaint;
Until we sacrifice so others may eat;
Until we right our wronged relationships;

Until we do our part to build the church for which
Christ died.

We often run from the demands of the gospel
While expecting our demands to be met.
Forgive our cowardice and neglect.
We repent of our posturing and pettiness.
Energize our discipleship that we may serve Thee
In the need of others, for Thy Kingdom's sake.
Amen.

13

Lord of our days,
We confess problems with personal honesty:
It is the other person with problems of anger and
greed.
Others are proud and deceitful, not we.
Our faults are never as bad as those of others.
We feature ourselves of superior character.
They are mistaken, not we.
Our opinion is the correct opinion.

All the ways of sin are known to us,
Especially pride.
Our haughtiness condemns us.
Our smugness makes us blind.
Our self-righteousness is an affront to honesty.

Forgive us for imagining ourselves above others
And for running from Thy judgment of us.
Humble us, for none is innocent of sin.
Through the Suffering Servant we pray. Amen.

14

Almighty God,
We confess to ambivalence
In appropriating what we have received.
We live by faith, but only so far,
We maintain hope, but only to a point.
We readily forgive if it appears a necessity.
We love compassionately when convenient.
We take missions seriously in special places,
We practice acceptance with certain persons.
We convey goodwill to those who return it.
We give sacrificially if it is not too costly.

Called to discipleship,
  we are bound by our selfishness.
Commissioned to gospel proclamation,
  we are barricaded by our narrowness.
Commanded to love,
  we are surrounded by reluctance.

Pardon, Lord, our pale performance;
Strengthen us to do Thy Will

With flexible faith and brave trust
For Jesus' sake. Amen.

15

Lord of our days,
Hold not our failures against us.
Hold our failures against Thy holy light,
That in the gleam of Thy healing grace
Our repentance may be sure,
Our forgiveness clear,
Thy never-changing love secure,
In the face of the faith
That holds us by Thy mighty hand. Amen.

PRAYERS
FOR
Worship

PASTORAL PRAYERS

In following the intent of the prayer Jesus gave His disciples to pray, the prayers in this chapter and the next have been subdivided into the following four sections:

> Adoration,
> Confession,
> Thanksgiving,
> Supplication.

As seems fitting in the prayer and appropriate to the local church, when a section of the Pastoral Prayer has been prayed, the worship leader may say "Through Jesus Christ our Lord" and the congregation may respond in unison with a vocal "Amen."

1

Our heavenly Father, Creator of all that is, who established order out of chaos, light out of darkness, and man from the dust of the earth; Create that spirit within us which would make us grateful for our creation and the life we know through faith in the Son of God.

Lord, we confess cankering sins of attitude; we tend to embrace regionalisms, ignoring the whole for the part that is comfortable; we adhere to personal creeds of questionable value so as to keep pleasure and deep joy continually confused; we enjoy censure and criticism that fits our mold for how people should behave; we extol the virtues of greedy and selfish people to our detriment. In short, we easily deceive ourselves through muddy thinking and paltry prejudices; we come to Thee acknowledging this distortion of our personhood. Grant us restoration, renewal, and the courage to submit our attitudes to the scrutiny of Higher Love.

We thank Thee for inspirations that have impelled

persons to create musically, artistically, or po-
etically; we thank Thee for challenges that have led
some persons to be missionaries in remote and difficult places; we thank Thee for dreams and visions
that stirred some parents to give so their children
could live fuller lives than their own; we thank Thee
for great causes that have led some persons to
forego personal comfort for the relief of suffering
humanity. Lord, we thank Thee for all good and
high and noble purposes that have used us and by
which we have been moved to right wrongs, create
beauty, and make our world a better place in which
to live.

We pray for those men and women at work in the
complexities of our social order: for schoolteachers
who seek to create an atmosphere of curiosity and
inspire pupils to learn; for police officers who help
the frightened with assistance and protect the angry
from themselves; for physicians who diagnose disease and use their skills to promote health; for fac-
tory workers and office personnel who perform
much needed but routine and repetitious tasks; for
legislators who enact laws and judges who interpret
them for the betterment of all. For all persons who
work long hours in honorable labor, in these and
the myriad other vocations, coping with pressures
of all kinds and degrees, we pray they may find
value both in what they do and in who they are.

For ourselves and all others, we pray that our
work may express the inward essence of who we are.

May we sense when to lay our labors down and rest; then, on the Sabbath, may we choose to worship and wait, so in Thy leading and love we be conformed to the image of Christ Jesus our Lord, in whose Name we pray. Amen.

2

Eternal God, our heavenly Father, who knowest all about us and lovest us unconditionally, who art always plenteous in mercy and generous in understanding, judging us not after the multitude of our sins but with perfect justice born of longsuffering patience; let our hearts be acceptable in Thy sight, O Lord, our strength and our Redeemer.

Father, we have failed one another and ourselves by passing on the other side of need. There are those we have shunned because their problems were too much for us and our problems seemed overwhelming. There are those we have walked beside but, because of their closeness, could not really see. There are those we failed to be kind to because they had never been kind to us. There are the aged, ignored and unwanted, for whom one hour of ours would have meant a period of increased personal worth. For our neglect and thoughtlessness, have mercy upon us, O Lord, and forgive us, we pray.

Our thanksgiving is for prayer: the prayers of our parents that follow us all our lives; the prayers of our friends that undergird us constantly; the prayers of our loved ones whose beauty of acceptance is affirmation itself; the prayers of our church where the community of the redeemed mirrors the will of the Father. We are encompassed about by spiritual powers; we draw on resources no person can vanquish; we are held in the grip of Invisible Love. Through private prayer, secret, vivid, life-changing,
we are sustained in our walk,
steadied in the faith,
secured in Thy fellowship,
and surrounded by cause for rejoicing.

We pray for those encompassed with the most perplexing problems, for whom no solution comes without pain and no alternatives without risk. Stabilize those who come from marriages where divorce becomes the most healthful way to survive and wrenched hearts separate. Undergird those who must face necessary surgery, terminal illness, or both. Calm those who on short notice must plan a funeral. Strengthen those who struggle to stay sober and those who in sobriety struggle to stay sane.

O Lord, when any of us are faced with one overriding option or agonizing decision, whatever it is, lead us to commit it to Thee, sure that in whatever we must do we will not be alone. Underneath are the everlasting arms; we are never a deserted people. All praise; we have the victory through our Lord Jesus Christ. Amen.

3

Gracious heavenly Father, who in storm art near to us, in distress our Comfort, in temptation's lure our Stay and Guide; shape us for worship, refining and remolding our inner lives after the precepts of Thy wisdom.

Forgive the sinful pride that sours our attitude toward one another and makes us think more highly of ourselves than we ought. With rationalizations, snap judgments, and surface evaluations, we deceive ourselves into believing things are only as we see them. Help us to probe beneath the surface, for often, as we seek more insight, we may find others in incalculable pain. Exploitation may reveal hunger and emptiness; manipulation, insecurity. Deception may reveal fear; infidelity, a deep desire to be loved.

Alas, the faults of others are our own, and our speedy tongues judge us sharply. Hear the guilt we bring to Thee as we repent and seek forgiveness. Be Thou Master of our hearts that our tongues would less pronounce judgments than blessings. Let patience and forbearance describe our attitudes. Even as Thou hast dealt kindly with us.

Lord, we are grateful for spontaneous and sensitive persons who revel in the ordinary and the unusual that we might otherwise miss. They point out:

the exquisite variety of snowflakes,
unguarded quips of children,
the joys of forking the earth to plant a garden,
wry phrases of illuminating wit,
a teenager's emerging skill in sports,
flashes of insight that merge intuition and knowledge,
a grandfather's comment on burning logs and resentments simultaneously,
the intricate design of layers beneath the head of toadstools.

We express appreciation that we can respond to Thy blessings found in the majestic flow of the seasons and the choice expressions of personality. Open us to the rich variety of this life that we may experience it to the depths and live it to the full.

Our petitions rise for the church universal, that she may be true to her high calling: preaching, teaching, and baptizing, in the Name of the Father, the Son, and the Holy Spirit. Where the work of missions is a struggle against ignorance and disease; where proclamation of the gospel is a struggle against idol worship in all its forms; where teaching the Bible is a struggle against language barriers and pagan customs; we pray for Thy Spirit to open doors and convict of sin for the salvation of many.

Let Thy Word bloom victorious from seed faithfully planted throughout the world. In this local church, let us be willing to tell what Christ means to us, not as burdensome duty but as spontaneous joy. May we never withhold sharing that which is most important to us, holds us secure in all storms, and gives us victory over sin and death; namely, our faith in the Lord Jesus Christ, through whom we pray. Amen.

4

Gracious Lord, Ruler of heaven and earth, Creator of the far-flung beauties of our universe and Author of the deep mysteries of life, as we brood over Thy incomparable majesty yet individual care for us, we are filled with a sense of awe and reverence.

The closer we draw to Thee, the more aware of our sins we become. Bogged in chosen rebellings of spirit, attitude, action, and thought, we ache in the chasm of sin's hollowness. We have been so insensitive and foolish. In haste to embrace the petty enticements and empty charms of our transgressions, momentarily we forgot our high calling in Christ Jesus; then we remembered, Thou art always with us. Cause again Thy flood of grace to cleanse and purify us as Thou hast promised.

Receive our prayers of gratitude for the gift of personality, for the uniqueness with which we are made and the giftedness with which others express who they are. For persons who cause us to think; for acquaintances who shoulder their share; for those who love us unconditionally; for children who teach us to wonder again; for our elders who show us what they consider life's essentials; we praise Thy Holy Name.

Help us to express the richness of our personalities in collaboration and coping so that together, in respect, friendship may blossom and self-expression be affirmed, even as we have known it in the nurture of Thy love.

We pray for persons who taste life's bitter edge and struggle to cope; for those who are hungry, undernourished and weak; for families where, through death or divorce, a parent is missing; for those numbed by depression born of grief; for those racked by disease, unable to afford adequate medical care.

O Thou who enterest every human situation with the light of choices, creativity, and the strength of acceptance; abide with those who feel life's sharp stinging blows and sustain them by their faith. So anchor their worth in Thee that amid provocations they may find light from above, strength from within and, through others, support from around them. When possible, permit us to be among the significant others who love the distressed and care for the unlovely in private deeds, born of secret prayer and a spiritual life hid with God in Christ. Amen.

5

O Lord our God, who knowest our needs before we ask and who longest to commune with us; we have come in glad anticipation to this time of worship. Let our meditation ponder not only Thy patient understanding of us, but how we may empathetically respond to others because of the value Thou givest us all.

We confess we often appear to be one thing on the outside and another on the inside. It is in us to pose and fake and give false impressions. We do not do this solely in the interest of peace-keeping and diplomacy. Much of it has to do with pretense, face-saving, and masking the true feelings we are afraid to express. We have not come to terms with either our pettiness or our rage, our privilege of response or our responsibility to be authentic.

Uncertain of ourselves, our worth, and our dignity, we are afraid of honest anger, of criticism that seeks to right wrongs and build constructively. As we voice our confession, hear also our desire to control anxious feelings rather than letting them control us. Enter our ambivalence, and lead us to honesty in attitude that squares with healthy self-expression and Thy peace.

We thank Thee for kindnesses that come to us unbidden:

for thoughtful words of appreciation;

for flowers that cheer the day;

for intercessory prayers that stabilize us in the storm;

for animals and pets that deepen our awareness;

for all good memories of warmth, security, and inspiration;

for phone calls that strengthen friendship;

for Scripture passages suddenly bursting streams of light into our souls.

We acknowledge all kindnesses, large or small, are channels of joy that enrich life and make it infinitely precious. Our gratitude overflows.

We pray for Thy help when we miss the point:

when we major on minors and magnify minutiae,

when we glory in the past, letting the present slip away,

when we lack financial discipline and try to exist on instant relief,

when we desire more than we can use and demand more than we deserve.

Call us, we pray, to a rugged self-examination that fosters maturity of insight and a Christian sense of priorities. Permit us to live with ourselves and all others so as to return good for evil, kindness for bitterness, gentleness for intransigence, and love for hate, where such response seems both wisest and best.

Without Thee, O Lord, we would lose all perspective for higher values, all taste for righteousness, all desire for holiness; therefore, we pray for discernment to give ourselves to causes worth living for and dying to perpetuate, in the spirit of Christ. Amen.

6

Lord, who found us when we were afar off and who holdest us ever near to Thee, what a difference this time of worship makes to us. We pause with all our burdens and pain in the realization of Thy majesty and mercy, awaiting Thy Word to us. Then we are not the same; we cannot explain it. We know Thee and we would know Thee better. Thou art our Creator who cherished us long before we cherished Thee, who brought us into being and provided for us the full cup of redemption. We praise Thee as through Thy Spirit we drink of it, for we are made close in all struggles, understood in all desires and joined in all hopes.

For ourselves we pray in the tenor and tone of a minor key: not for what we fail to have, but for what we fail to do with what we have; not for lack of opportunity, but for lack of persistent courage to make opportunities; not for basic necessities, but for lack of multiplying basic provisions in the ministry of sharing. For ours are sins of timidity, Lord, of complacency in the midst of opportunity and lethargy in the face of need.

Forgive us. Turn us from the dissonance of selfishness to a full harmony of prayer, praise, and service. Let us go forth changed by what we know of Thee and what by Thy Holy Spirit we might aid to fruition in others. Hasten the day.

We are thankful for the way Truth holds sway in our hearts when we tend to part from Thy precepts. Many times we have desired the tents of wickedness, only to realize that a day in Thy courts is better than a thousand in any other abode. We have desired what did not belong to us, only to be met by the assurance we belong to Thee and our position is adequate. We have wanted to sever our closest relationships, only to realize we are joined in Thy unchanging love and have been brought to clearer light. We could endlessly recount our blessings wrought by Thy higher wisdom. Now we rejoice with gratitude. Praise to Thee, God of our salvation.

We pray for those who, for whatever reason, were passed by when they had planned a marriage, expected a raise, anticipated an award, qualified for the team, deserved a promotion, applied for membership. As we ponder this experience so common to all, gather our disappointments into Thy love. As seems best, help us to redefine our goals, rechannel our energies, and taking fresh courage, try again. We pray this in the triumphant Name of Jesus who transformed the tragedy of an unwarranted death into ultimate victory over sadness and sin, by the power of God. Amen.

7

O Thou who art the source of all our joy and the
hope of our lives, whose grace encompasseth us and
whose love never departeth from us; endow our
worship with the power of Thy Spirit, that our lives
may be shaped from within to express outwardly the
glory of Thy Name.

Lord, we are guilty of detached concern for man-
kind. We flippantly ridicule others, unmindful of
the true state of their private struggle. We harbor
attitudes of distrust because we do not want to over-
look idiosyncrasies and accept others as they are.
We run from the terminally ill, the unfed, the incarcerated, because our subjective feelings bother
us too much. We often do not want to be bothered
with the plight of the world's hungry, or the struggle
for world peace: we have done our work and want to
be left alone. Our consciences accuse us, our prejudices reveal us. Our failure to go the second mile
of concern betrays not so much our neglect of
others as our poverty of soul. From these and all
other distance-keeping maneuvers, merciful Lord,
deliver us.

We are grateful, Father, for all in life that speaks of
dependability:
    the reliable ebb and flow of the seasons;
    the solid-rock relationship with a friend;
    the dignity derived from work, honestly done;

the steady movement of the day;
the stabilizing comfort of the Scriptures;
the refreshment of adequate sleep;   .
the intangible but underlying strength of faith.
For all that has been proven, tried, and true, in
values, relationships, knowledge, and beauty, we
express thanksgiving to Thee, who changest not and
art from everlasting to everlasting the same.

We request, that to the degree we know suffering,
we might also know Thy sustenance. O Lord, facili-
tate the emergence of courage in our needy hour.

Some spirits here were wounded this week by un-
kind words and thoughtless attitudes heaped on
them, or by them; forgive them. Some lives were
overwhelmed in sorrow by a hospitalization, a freak
accident, a death; comfort them. Some knew job-
lessness, and others, the alienation that comes with
loneliness; renew them. Some took steps toward facing themselves and their lifestyles, their bottled emotions and justified anger; mature them. Some were
made joyous by closer family ties, children excelling
at school, parents and grandparents closer in adult
interaction. Seal their joy.

So weave into the tapestry of our lives golden
strings of self-acceptance and authentic faith that,
when dark threads mark the journey through our
days, the steady colors of Thy abiding love and caring grace will weave around their sorrow, meaning
of such magnitude as to bring good from the struggle, strength from the pain, and endurance from

the battle; in the mighty Name of Jesus, we pray. Amen.

8

Almighty and everlasting Father, who lovest us beyond our comprehending and carest for us beyond our understanding; calm our anxious cares and quiet our stress-ridden minds. Open us to Thy strength born of stillness, Thy wisdom born of meditation, and Thy courage born of the Word, as we worship Thee in spirit and in truth.

We purpose to follow Thee, Lord. That we choose to do so a long way off is an integral part of our rebellion.

While not fully endorsing some moral laxities, we tend never to oppose them and by silent consent permit others to fall in their grip. While not fully opposing the work of the church, many through inabsentia allegiance permit its effectiveness to wane and its possibilities to deteriorate in their lives. Through neglect we often fail Thee and ourselves, and we seek Thy pardon. When we cloud the picture of Thy purposes for us by

haphazard care of our souls,
scant attention paid to others,
damaging criticism passed routinely,
vain worship of power or self,

secret conceits of our own importance,
nursing temptations till we surrender to them,
we pray Thou wilt look with mercy upon us, forgive
our sins, and renew a right spirit within us.

We express our praise for days that have been
blessed by excellence:
>   for workmanship of fine quality;
>   for craftmanship that expresses personal concern;
>   for scientific achievements that bless all persons;
>   for integrity in relationships that spawns trust;
>   for extraordinary service that renders break-
>   through results;
>   for monumental dedication that stabilizes institu-
>   tions;
>   for sacrifice freely given, to raise standards of liv-
>   ing physically, mentally, and spiritually.

For these and all other expressions of the highest
that is in us, we acknowledge deep gratitude, O
Lord, and especially for Thy highest expression of
love, Christ Jesus.

We pray for all confused interpersonal relationships
in which we are concerned, realizing there are
those we never understood because we never took
the time, just as there are those who use us and
whom we have used, because of pride and a false
sense of the basic worth of persons. We pray for all
families, including our own, who mistake
>   possessions for self-esteem,
>   children for security,

pleasure for deep joy,
manipulation for authentic relationships,
and overintellectualizing for faith in God.
Cause us to probe beneath the surface of what we
do, and, if we find there any mistaken intent, to
commit it to Thee and correct the error of our ways.
We pray in the Name of the Christ, whose life
changed all history and whose redemption has
changed us into seekers of Thy will. Amen.

9

Would that this day we could express the magnitude
of our love for Thee, O Lord of Hosts. Words fail
us, yet our hearts lift up rich gratitude formed in
humility and shaped by worship. Allow us to love
Thee with all that we are and hope to be, and our
neighbors as ourselves. Thou art our God and
greatly to be praised. There is none other beside
Thee! Glory to Thy Name!

We ask forgiveness for laxities in our personal Christian pilgrimage: for our failure to sift through events
to their deeper meanings; for failure to trust because
trusting is difficult; for seeking forgiveness without
forgiving first; for ignoring the Scriptures because
we are too busy; for failure to give the anonymous
gift of help known only to Thee and the recipient;

for requesting of Thee more than we can use and wanting more than we need.

Father, transient concerns have blighted our spiritual maturity. Possessions get in our way, busyness robs our time for contemplation, and selfishness darkens our devotional lives. Orient our priorities by Thy Word. Forgive us, we pray. Let the Christ of history become the Lord of our lives, through the power of the Holy Spirit.

We thank Thee that in the wake of the storm that passed by we were left unharmed. By health maintained and work well done we are enriched. For friends, who through the passing of the years grow deeper and richer as our lives intertwine, we feel doubly blessed. For colorful seasons that pass across field and plain, causing to come alive with beauty the most common plant, we exclaim with joy. That beneath us are the everlasting arms; that above us is the watchcare of God; that around us is a community of the redeemed; that within us is the surety of faith and a love that will not let us go; we express abounding gratitude.

In all these goodnesses, from sunrise to sunset and all through the night, we express our thankfulness. May we do so through all the days of our lives and then beyond.

We pray for those removed from the mainstream of life who feel separated: the orphaned and the retarded, the alcoholic and the mentally ill, the hospitalized and the incarcerated, the bedfast and the drug-addicted, those in the military, and the avowedly promiscuous. At times we all feel aloneness and apartness from all others. We search for security also. Cause all those to whom alienation is critical to know that as they seek Thee they will find Thee. Thou dost not leave us or forsake us, and through the valley of the shadow of deepest depression, Thou art with us. Let the anxiety of separation be met by the truth that Thou art ever seeking us. Give to us all faith to believe in that of Thee which we can understand, and to trust with brave faith in that of Thee which we do not understand. Through the Son of God. Amen.

10

Gracious heavenly Father, from whom every goodness flows, all light emanates, and all life-centering peace comes; look with mercy upon us as we worship Thee. With steadiness of attention, resolve of heart and clarity of thought, enable us to be edified in an encounter with the living Christ, our Savior and Redeemer. Through Thy Spirit convict us of our transgressions and by Thy power make us clean and whole again, and we will be whole indeed.

We confess we often carry to excess our reactions to the stress we feel. Then through rationalization, we justify overindulgence. Discouragement tempts us to despair; anger, to depression; tension, to anxiety; bereavement, to withdrawal; incapacitation, to self-pity; rejection, to loneliness.

We are not always aware of ways we would justify our behavior, but encountering these subtle turns of mind today, we bring them to Thee in confession, just as they are: failures on our part to trust. Thou alone art worthy of our highest affection and loyalty. We ponder that as an earthly father longs to give good gifts to his children, how much more does our Father in heaven long to reward us, the highest of all creation, His obedient children. Lead us to trust Thee enough to be done with our pitiful excesses of faithlessness.

Our lives are endowed by small gifts from nature that sensitize and deepen our spirits: the gentle drops of lazy rain, the uplifting mood of fragrant flowers, the vibrant songs of melodious birds, and the dew-filled veins of roadside grass.

Our lives are deepened and matured by significant relationships in the human family: the warm acceptance of loved ones, the infectious laughter of children, the deep ties of friendship, and the choice camaraderie of colleagues.

Let these and all Thy blessings shape us into persons more prone to giving than receiving and more given to gratitude than complaining. With great joy we thank Thee, our God, for the cheerful and limitless enrichment of the passage of our days.

We pray for those who would rather not
  go to school,
    go to work,
      go to the doctor,
       go to church,
        go home.
We intercede for those who resent
  their jobs,
    their economic status,
      their parents,
       their suffering,
        their appearance,
        their birth.
Our heart cries out for those who know the stifling trap of unreleased anger. We pray for those to whom a hard edge of resentment is a way of life, for whom others are half a nuisance to be endured and who feel helpless, alone, and afraid.

How is it you come to us, Lord, and lift us out of the pit of self-pity and bestow on us meaning for life and patience with mysteries we cannot explain? Is it not through faith? By the power of Thy Holy Spirit, fill those who are fearful and alienated with an experience of life-altering grace. Help Thy servants in the community of the redeemed to examine our attitudes lest in doubt we falter by poor judgment, express less than we believe, and live less than we know. In the Redeemer's Name we pray. Amen.

PRAYERS
FOR
Worship

PRAYERS FOR
SPECIAL OCCASIONS

Palm Sunday

Lord of life, who in the turning of all seasons changest not, and whose watchcare over us, though majestic with all holy thought, is personal, penetrating, and abiding; accept our praise as we come rejoicing. "Hosanna! Blessed is He who comes in the Name of the Lord. All praise in heaven and glory in the earth!"

Hear our confession, for we admit a willingness to proclaim Thee Lord of our lives today, and abandon Thee tomorrow. So easily would we follow the crowd as it makes and breaks heroes. Our divided effort to serve two masters at the same time splinters us, and we are caught in desperate straits.

We are guilty of kind deeds from selfish motives, advertising our sacrifice for personal glory, and using others to better our position. We are unable to pass by these transgressions lightly. Let us love Thee wholeheartedly. We want to be done with the transitory, the counterfeit and the self-defeating. Stir our hearts to repentance. Grant Thy gracious forgiveness as we begin again.

We are thankful for worship's celebrative moments: for insights of self that cause us to rejoice inside at Thy grace; for moments of joy that cause us to sing in unison of Thy love; for unplanned moments of prayer when we gladly testify to Thy watchcare over us. We are recipients of a fellowship in faith. We are bound together in common concerns representing Christ to one another and to the world.

In this high privilege we are humbled and challenged. We covet the responsibility. We rejoice in the trust. We pray for strength to do our part. Praise be to God!

We are mindful this Palm Sunday that as on that first triumphal entry many persons did not know Thee, or if they knew Thee, they followed afar off. We pray for the silent followers; the doubtful followers; the followers who give up too soon. Not all of us are as strong in the faith as we would like to be. We know the pattern worship takes, the customs and rituals, but often we are far away and unconcerned. Doing our part in the distance, we become even more detached. Then spiritual matters are forgotten.

Restore unto those who know the pattern of escape, a thirst for the water of life. Based on the deepest they know Thee, urge them to seek again that depth of relationship, through Christ our Lord, who in the midst of every crowd always finds us.

Good Friday

A Prayer Concerning the Crucifixion

O Lord, who art more concerned for our salvation than we are, who through suffering hast shown us the way to Thee; accept now our prayer of remembrance beside the lonely cross on which Christ died. We are staggered by the paradox of Crucifixion, where all that was pure bore every impurity, where all that was sacred and human in its highest expression encountered all that was unsacred and inhuman in its lowest expression, and where all goodness was put to the final test.

We request insight and perception as we examine the meaning of that singular death. Allow that we might this day see the death of the Savior as it was for Christ and must be for us. We return to Calvary where the supreme drama of the ages unfolded itself in fury and unleashed its agony in pain. He who was pre-existent with the Father and Chief Agent in creation, was faithful unto death, even death on a cross.

We thank Thee, Lord, with contrite hearts that Jesus Christ, without spot or blemish, accepted the full load of sin's sting and bore it for our sake. We are humbled, for we are intimately involved. Shape anew our priorities in the awareness of that costly sacrifice. Lead us to confront ignorance, disease, poverty, and pain, with the cross ever before us and the sure hope of ultimate victory undergirding us, by the blood of the everlasting covenant, the Crucified Son. Amen.

Easter

O Lord, our God, who feelest the affliction of our sin and the guilt of our transgressions more deeply than we, yet lovest us unstintingly above all that we are able to say and do; we are thankful that Thy mercy is not dependent on the profundity of our thought, the purity of our lives, or the perfection of our conduct. Stir us by the power of Thy presence to pray and sing with gladness, in the worship of resurrection joy.

We confess to divided efforts trying to find coherence for our lives; we run to meet passing fortune and come home to count our losses; we follow paths not of Thy purposes but of our choosing, to their dead end; we grope for life's meaning in lectures and books, ignoring private prayer and the Book; we look to others for self-assurance, afraid of the truth that worth comes from Thee and rises from within.

How long will it be before we learn to trust Thee, Lord?

Forgive our scattered wonderings and splintered searchings. Let us know Thee in prayer, where to find Thee is to place life in its highest perspective, and to find ourselves extending that knowledge in Christian service.

We express gratitude for profound lessons in simple forms:

    Rainbow colors in the waterfall;

    The intricate beauty of spider webs;

    A sunset after the rain;

    The pure trust of children;

    The refining lessons of age;

    The difference between the ornate and the adequate;

    The silent beauty of growth and maturity;

    The surety of love.

Sensitize us to the simplicities of life's rhythms even in distressing times. We are thankful for all that we see of Thee in the fabric of every passing day.

This Easter, when many of us are so happy to be with our families in church, we intercede on behalf of those who never make it to church but whom Thou enfoldest with Thy love all the same. May Thy special mercies attend the grossly retarded and brain-damaged children; the paraplegics and iron-lung patients; the chronically psychotic and acutely alcoholic; the sufferers of contagious diseases and the bedfast elderly; the deaf, dumb, illiterate, and the prisoners in solitary confinement. Endow their families and the doctors, nurses, orderlies, guards, and teachers that attend them, with unusual sensitivity and patient understanding.

May those who do the thankless tasks be reminded that as they serve others in Christ's Name, they serve Christ, and may those who are served feel as much of Thy love through others as they are capable of knowing.

As we face the mystery of suffering in the painful corners of life, remind us again of the meaning of Christ's death and resurrection over all the forces of evil. In His Name, we pray. Amen.

Mother's Day

O Lord, our God, whose love cannot be measured, whose holiness is beyond finite understanding, whose greatness covers heaven and earth, reaching the far corners of the universe; Thou alone art worthy of our worship and praise. In awe we bow before Thee. We beseech Thee to stir our humbled hearts into visions of response, fitting and appropriate for Thy praise. Then do with us as Thou wilt.

We confess this day, parents and children alike, that we are imperfect and often short with one another. In homes where mistakes have been made and personalities injured, for whatever reason, we ask courage to acknowledge errors and sensitivity to express forgiveness. If we never forgive our parents their failures, our children their rebellings, and our mates their weaknesses, we wrap ourselves in vengeance and tie the knot that binds us to immaturity and self-hate. In accepting Thy forgiveness, hasten

אנכי ה'   לא תרצח
לא יהיה   לא תנאף
לא תשא   לא תגנב
זכור את   לא תענה
כבר את   לא תחמד

In Remembrance

TREADWELL-NORRIS FUNERAL CHAPEL

2944 WALNUT GROVE ROAD

MEMPHIS, TENNESSEE

 ❧ ❧

COSMOPOLITAN FUNERAL HOME

1900 UNION AVENUE

MEMPHIS, TENNESSEE

us to make amends with all others, forgiving them repeatedly as we would want to be forgiven.

For all mothers who find children a shared joy and a wanted delight, we express a great sense of appreciation. If there was one in this world who with unconditional love accepted and nurtured us, we give thanks.

For all roots of motherhood that established in us values and ideals patterned after God's law and love;

For all abilities to accept others and feel accepted and wanted ourselves;

For all sensitivities to gentle, small, and sensitive things;

For that sense of continuing faith and belief that our mothers displayed so devotedly;

For the pivotal interaction of brother and sister, and lessons learned in growing up that undergirded us for living together in marriages of our own;

We say, Thy goodness through our mothers has been an anchor to us, a sure sign of Thy continuous watchcare. Our gratitude overflows.

In our families where children emerge, impressionable and growing, we ask that an integration of personality may be theirs, marking them as healthy, known for kindness, sensitivity, and noble ideals. In the exercise of parenthood may discipline not be marked by inconsistency. May it always be quickly followed by the love that embraces the person while disapproving errant behavior. Grant wisdom and discernment to those who are charged with responsibility, that they may cling to and embrace in their families all that is of precious, growing worth, and sound maturity. May all the days of our lives be marked by seeking and promoting healthy relationships.

For those older persons in illness and confinement, for whom simply making it through the day without pain is an exception, our voices rise in intercession. Grant them courage, presence of mind and a resilience of spirit that transcends declining health.

Provide each of us a sense of belonging to the family of God, that we may always be young in commitment, adult in service, and old in trusting Thee; through Christ our Lord. Amen.

Father's Day

Almighty God, who hast set in motion the universe, carving the land out of the sea, placing the galaxies and planets in orbit; receive now our humble praise and glad worship for that which sustains us, though we comprehend it not. Because Thou hast first loved us, we now love Thee, and in reverence, humble ourselves before Thee, O Lord of hosts.

As parents, we confess that we have misunderstood and been misunderstood. We have misinterpreted and been misinterpreted. We have let frustration anger us and allowed secondary behavior to seem primary. We, who love our children with all our hearts, have often erred when trying to do right. Forgive our failures; bless our best efforts; nurture our children into godly men and women.

As children, we confess we become impatient with our parents and their outdated, outmoded, and old-fashioned ideas. In that evaluation we may be right, we may be wrong; but, Lord, do not let it corrode our respect for one another. Help us to honor our parents where honor is due and obey when it is our reasonable service.

As fathers, we confess that the demands upon our time have often divided us and caused us to be away from home. We confess the need to provide and the privilege to parent are difficult to keep in balance. We know all the years of our children's lives are formative and we are pivotal in that formation. Mold our character and multiply our patience so that time spent with our children will be of the finest quality and lasting worth.

We breathe a Father's Day prayer, Lord, of gratitude for the worthy memory of stalwart fathers who were men of the Bible and who were often found in the private counsels of prayer; for fathers who labored industriously, toiling long hours by the sweat of their brows, trying to keep home and family together; for fathers who were sensitive to our needs, who, with economy of words and wisdom of the years, spoke only the word we needed and did not belabor the point; for fathers who understood us well enough to relinquish us to our own successes and failures, yet guided us steadily as guidance was needed.

We need strong men, Lord. Raise them up in our midst if it please Thee, and grant them moral fiber to stand for truth and goodness when all about them tempts toward the counterfeit and transitory. Undergird those fathers who are separated or divorced, endow them with a strong measure of Thy love that goes on accepting when hurts divide. Grant us all that sense of oughtness and ability in relationships that marks the maturity of wise men. We would learn from one another. For those who serve as father substitutes in crucial times, we ask a measure of Thy understanding and an astute sense of Thy leadership.

Lord, in our families, let us seek peaceful accord in decision-making, respect in discipline, and honor regardless of our differences. May our love for Thee be mirrored in our affection for one another, through Christ, our Redeemer. Amen.

Christmas

O Lord, whose ways are higher than our ways, whose thoughts are higher than our thoughts, and whose love proclaimed Messiah's birth through the Babe at Bethlehem; we worship Thee.

This sacred season of the year is pervaded by possessiveness. We confess being given to covetousness. Lured by commercialism, we are often anxious and vain. Forgetful of those who have little, we splurge on ourselves. We often give most to those least in need.

Our priorities become confused when we forget the Lord in the manger,
   the life He lived,
     the teachings He taught,
      the death He endured.
Forgive the greed, shortsightedness, and stubbornness that stifle our lives and clog our spirits. Lead us in right paths of new commitment for Thy Name's sake.

Our families are strengthened to be together again at this Christmas season. We remember loved ones with whom we shared Christmases past; a parent, a mate, a daughter, a son, a brother, a sister, a treasured friend. Now we rejoice that they are at peace, joined more intimately with Thee, and we are thankful for the light they brought us. Let us never underestimate the power of Christian influence.

On a deeper level, we view the presence of Christ as Incarnation: God with us. Robed in human flesh, Deity made the full journey from cradle to cross, then crowned it with Resurrection and Ascension. Thou hast shown us the way; we rejoice in the grace by which we too may walk that way in faith.

We are surrounded by the technicolor of the season, a massive display of tinsel and trappings wrapped in commercialism. Permit us to envision the clear purity of that holy light which shone the first Christmas Eve, causing all other lights to be seen in appropriate perspective. Move us with the profundity of a lowly crib in a barn, humble shepherds from the fields, wise men from distant lands, all participating in the birth of Messiah. Permit our gift-giving to be in the spirit of adoration and wonderment.

O God of the manger, become God of our minds and Lord of our affections. Fill our hearts with kindness, our actions with caring, our spirits with gentleness, so we might become more like Thee, and more of what we ought to be through the Prince of Peace. Amen.

PRAYERS FOR Worship

OFFERTORY PRAYERS

1

Father,
We reap where others have sown.
We gather where others have planted.
We receive where others have sacrificed.
Therefore, allow our portion of giving
To go on blessing those in need
Whom we have never met,
Until Thy kingdom comes. Amen.

2

Lord,
May we follow the example of the Master
Who gave, withholding nothing,
That we might live
To share everything
Through His Name. Amen.

3

Father,
We celebrate the possibilities of this offering.
Use it to accomplish great deeds,
Going where we cannot go,
Nurturing to faith
And maturing in grace
All who hear Thy Word
And call on Thy Holy Name. Amen.

4

Father, through whom we are enabled to do all that
    we do,
And through whom all we have been given has
    come.
Receive now this portion of Thy bounty to us.

Allow our giving to match our dedication;
Permit our sacrifice to match our sincerity;
Increase our service to match our intentions;
For the building of Thy Kingdom
And the glory of Thy Son. Amen.

5

Because we cannot claim generosity
  if in giving we share only a penance;
Because we cannot claim sacrifice
  if in giving we share only a portion;
Because we cannot claim stewardship
  if in giving we withhold the best part;

Permit us to give to Thee, O Lord,
Our money and ourselves,
Continuously with no abatement;
Unreservedly with no hesitation;
Exuberantly with no small delight;
Because such giving is pattern for joy
And pathway to peace. Amen.

6

Almighty God,
Through whom all life emerges
And all personality is born,
Prod us to share the unique abilities
With which we are endowed,

Including the measure of money
Generously entrusted to us,
That, in sharing both gifts,
Personality and peace may multiply,
Through the power of the Holy Spirit. Amen.

7

O Lord our God,
We desire that this offering express
Careful and willing sharing on our part
With fruitful and merciful blessing on Thy part,
As together we seek to build
Thy kingdom among the nations
And Thy will among all peoples;
Through Christ, the King of Kings. Amen.

8

Father of all good gifts,
We cannot outgive Thee.
Here is a portion of our possessions we are prone to
    keep.
We have other uses for this money.
They all pale in the light of our gratitude to Thee.

Let this be our joy.
For Jesus' sake. Amen.

9

Lord, our God,
Let joy grip all who give
And gratitude, all who receive.
May all littleness of spirit,
Appearance of greed,
And expression of vanity
Not be found among us.
May this offering be found
In the place of greatest need
For the spread of Thy Will
And the appropriation of Thy love. Amen.

10

Lord of the vineyard of life,
We who have much now give our share.
We who have little now give our share.
Great sum or small,
So utilize our gifts in the work of the church
That the seed of Thy Word, once planted,
May in due season bring forth
Living fruit in changed lives. Amen.

11

Father,
We who want more than we have,
Covet more than we deserve,
And spend more than we earn,
Approach this offering with less than joy
And this prayer with less than content.

Forgive us our selfish ways,
That we may give with generosity
And pray with sincerity,
Allowing this money to be more for others
Than it was to us
And permitting us to be truer to Thee
Than we have been to ourselves. Amen.

12

Generous Lord,
May we give because giving is like Thee.
May we share
Because truth is multiplied by sharing.
May we do this
Because Thou lovest a cheerful giver

And Thou art like that with us.
Through Christ our Lord. Amen.

13

Lord of life,
Help us to maintain the vital balance
Between material necessities
And spiritual blessings
That releases us by faith
To generosity in stewardship
And trust in love. Amen.

14

Remind us as we give, O Lord,
Of an open cross upon a lonely hill,
Where all the generosity and love
Of a compassionate heavenly Father
Culminated in the willing sacrifice
Of the obedient Son for our salvation.
Then may we give,
Humbled in gratitude,
Determined in generosity,

And dedicated in commitment,
To sacrifice in Thy service
And live in Thy joy. Amen.

15

He gives best who prays best
Seeing God in all about,
For giving is the hand of God
That praying reaches out. Amen.

PRAYERS
FOR
Worship

LITANIES AND
AFFIRMATIONS

A Litany of God's Law
Based on Psalm 19

Minister. In what does the soul delight?
People. *The law of the Lord is perfect, reviving the soul.*
Minister. In what word is the wisdom of life?
People. *The testimony of the Lord is sure, making wise the simple.*
Minister. What truth makes the heart glad?
People. *The precepts of the Lord are right, rejoicing the heart.*
Minister. When it is difficult to see the way, where is our light?
People. *The commandment of the Lord is pure, enlightening the eyes.*
Minister. What attitude of respect toward God is everlasting?
People. *The fear of the Lord is clean, enduring for ever.*
Minister. Is the worship of God to be desired?
People. *The ordinances of the Lord are true, and righteous altogether;*
More to be desired than fine gold,
Sweeter also than the drippings of the honeycomb.

Minister. Remember, by the ordinances of the
Lord His servants are warned;
In keeping them is great reward.

People. *Let the words of my mouth and the*
meditation of my heart
Be acceptable in Thy sight, O Lord, my
rock and my redeemer.

An Affirmation of Faith

The basis of faith is desire.
The beginning of faith is commitment.
The heartbeat of faith is trust.
The privilege of faith is sharing.
The beauty of faith is acceptance.
The hope of faith is belief in God.
The joy of faith is the peace of God.
The reward of faith is the presence of God.
The focus of faith is the Son of God.
With all diligence, therefore,
I will keep the faith
By which I am kept
Through the Lord Jesus Christ. Amen.

A Litany on
the Passing of Another Week

Minister. We have lived another week and erred
toward others in many ways.

People.   We have not always listened. We tend to
          manipulate. We even dehumanize and
          are not aware of it.

Minister.   We have lived another week and erred in
          many ways toward God.

People.   We have failed to seek the will of God.
          We have forgotten to love God through
          the needy.
          We began and ended our days and failed
          to pray.

Minister.   We have lived another week and erred in
          many ways toward ourselves.

People.   We have harbored hate. The sun set on
          our anger; we even punished ourselves
          as if to avoid God's judgment. In the
          battle between the good and the
          questionable, we embraced our
          doubts.

Minister.   Let God do the punishing and the
          forgiving. God hears your confession
          and freely pardons. If you receive
          another seven days, how will you live
          them?

People.   We will live each day as forgiven persons,
          more sensitive to others
              more open to God
                  and more honest with ourselves.

Minister.   May our resolve become reality
              as God opens the door
                  of another week.

All.   Amen.

A Litany of Human Personality

Minister. May we express our gratitude to God for the varying expressions of personality that surround and enrich our lives:

People. For aggressive, self-confident, and energetic persons, who move us from inactivity to service.

Minister. *You are the light of the world. Let your light so shine before men that they may see your good works and glorify your Father which is in heaven.*

People. For quick-witted persons, who tell tales, pinpoint the humorous, and observe the amusing in the human situation.

Minister. *A merry heart maketh a cheerful countenance.*

People. For kind and gentle persons, the sum total of whose good deeds are known only to Thee, but whose expression of Thy love endears them to all they meet.

Minister. *But when thou doest alms, let not thy left hand know what thy right hand doeth . . . and thy Father which seeth in secret shall reward thee openly.*

People. For talented and creative persons who flood our lives with new ideas, originality, and insight.

Minister. *For unto whom much is given, of him shall much be required.*

People.   For persons of unusual faith, who see the deeper currents of life. They cause us to face the mystery of God and search out meaning for our days.

Minister. *Looking unto Jesus, the author and finisher of our faith.*

People.   For quiet, humble persons who are not greatly talented, but who have mastered the art of an affirming word. They make us feel good about being who we are.

Minister. *A word fitly spoken is like apples of gold in pictures of silver.*

All.   Lord, release the uniqueness that best expresses who we are. Affirm in us all that is good and winsome, and pleasing to Thee. For our good and Thy glory. Amen.

An Affirmation of Salvation

We believe in a God of free will,
Who called us into being,
Created us a little lower than the angels,
And gave us freedom to accept or reject His love.

We believe in a God of salvation
Who came to us in Christ Jesus, the unique Son.
He was born as a babe in Bethlehem.
In His youth He was a carpenter in Nazareth.

As an adult He taught and healed,
    preached and prayed,
        and was friend to the friendless.
As a young man He was killed.
He died on a cross like any common criminal.
In His death, He paid the penalty of sin for all
    persons.
The third day after His burial,
He arose victorious over sin and death.
He now intercedes before the Father in glory
For all who call His Name.

We hold that the meaning of life is found
In a faith relationship to Jesus Christ.
We submit to His rule of love in our hearts
Now and forever.

A Litany of Praise
Based on Psalm 24:7–10

People.   *Lift up your heads, O ye gates,*
          And be ye lift up, ye everlasting doors,
          And the King of glory shall come in.
Minister. *Who is the King of glory?*
People.   *The Lord strong and mighty,*
          The Lord mighty in battle,
          The Lord of hosts, He is the King of
             glory.

Minister. Lift up your hearts in prayer:
Lift up your voices in praise.
Let your eyes rise in expectation,
And your hands in exultation,
For the Lord has drawn near,
And dwells among us.
People. We lift them up. Amen.

An Affirmation of Faith

We believe in the presence of God,
His nearness to protect,
His love to comfort,
His law to obey;
His Spirit to guide,
His Word to instruct,
His hope to strengthen,
His Grace to share
Through Jesus, the Son,
Who makes God's presence vivid
Through His holy life,
   His painful death,
      His victorious resurrection,
         and continual intercession,
            on our behalf
               before the Father
                  in heaven.

Our lives are rooted in this gospel.
This is mystery but it is also truth.
This we believe.

A Litany of Praise
Based on Psalm 100 (RSV)

Minister. We have gathered in the Name of the
Lord
What is your response?

People. *Make a joyful noise to the Lord, all the
lands!*
Serve the Lord with gladness!
Come into his presence with singing!

Minister. Why do you take this time for the Lord?

People. *Know that the Lord is God!*
It is he that made us; we did not.
*We are his people, and the sheep of his
pasture.*

Minister. How will you worship the Lord?

People. *We will enter his gates with thanksgiving
And his courts with praise.*
*We will give thanks to him, and bless his
name.*

Minister. What is the basis for this outpouring of
praise?

All. *The Lord is good; his mercy is everlasting,
And his truth endureth to all generations.*
Amen.

An Affirmation of the Holy Spirit

We believe the Holy Spirit is the Spirit of God.
The Holy Spirit is completely God,
Not a fragmented part of God.
The Spirit is God totally relating to us:
   in inspiration and guidance,
   in illumination and judgment,
   in redemption and intercession,
     unlimited, unbound, and unpredictable.

The Holy Spirit brings God's truth to us,
And brings us to the truth about ourselves.

The Holy Spirit guides us in our understanding of
   God,
Clarifies our realization of Christ, and
Informs our pilgrimage of faith.

The Holy Spirit, forever present,
Undergirds us in the flailing winds of temptation,
Plants joy in us beyond worldly comprehension,
Chastises us when we deny God,
Calms our inner turmoil with holy peace,
And shapes our subconscious in slumber
For service when we are awake.

The Holy Spirit clarifies the truths of the Bible
So we may apply them

To the painful hurts and appalling injustices
Of a splintered and jaded world.
By the Holy Spirit, truth is sealed in our hearts,
Guiding us into a knowledge of God
That shapes us for life on earth
And prepares us for heaven above.

We believe in the Holy Spirit,
For by that Spirit we perceive the will of God.

A Litany of Gratitude for Thought

All.   Lord and Creator,
People.   We are grateful for good minds
             That help us grasp knowledge and find
                truth.
Minister. We are grateful for free will,
People.   Enabling us to choose our own direction.
Minister. We are grateful for memory,
People.   Whereby we can cherish the poignant
                and profound in review.
Minister. Through imagination,
People.   We can dream and picture our ideals.
Minister. Through insight,
People.   We can analyze significant experiences.
Minister   Through conscience prayerfully
                sharpened,

People.   We can choose fulfilling behavior and
              shun the counterfeit.
Minister.   Through intuition,
People.   We can sense the appropriate time to do,
              or refrain from doing our part.
Minister.   Lord, truly we are fearfully and
              wonderfully made,
              Indeed a little lower than the angels,
People.   And crowned with personality
              That permits us to reflect on our
              behavior.
              We thank Thee, Lord, for the very
              thought of Thee
              And how that knowledge is integrated
              With our sense of worth,
              And Thy seeking love. Amen.

PRAYERS
FOR
Worship

BENEDICTIONS

1

God undergirds you.
God sustains you.
God empowers you.
God strengthens you.
God loves you.
Live for God,
Because you desire nothing less
And you request nothing more;
Through His Son, our Savior. Amen.

2

Across your path this week
May walk more challenge,
More sorrow, or more fulfillment
Than any other week of your life.
The next seven days may also be a routine repeat
Of a hundred unspectacular weeks
You have known before.

See each day as precious.
Accept each day as gift.
Live each day to the full.
For pervading every moment
Is the Spirit of God,
Working in you
To accomplish His will. Amen.

3

Allow the strength of God to sustain you,
The wisdom of God to instruct you,
The hand of God to protect you,
The shield of God to defend you,
The Spirit of God to lead you,
The Son of God to redeem you,
Until by the grace of God,
We see Him face to face. Amen.

4

Go forth with steady step
As you face the days ahead.
Live, certain that in many ways,
God provides faith for darkened hours,
Courage in despairing nights,
And calm in depressing circumstances.

Revel in your joys,
Recall your blessings,
Walk in the Light.

So live, that if among days it were your last,
It would represent
   in living, your finest,
   in loving, your Savior,
   in dying, a final benediction of noble character,
   through Jesus Christ our Lord. Amen.

5

The grace, peace, and love
Of the triune God
Protect, defend, and empower you
To stand in the tempests,
Walk through the storms,
And abide in the light;
Through the victorious faith
Found in the regnant Christ. Amen.

6

Practice the presence of Christ.
Ponder the Scriptures.
Pray daily in private.
Serve others in Christ's Name.

To widows and orphans, the poor and oppressed,
Withhold no good deed, spiritual or financial.

As you live this way,
You will find those most needy of God,
You will find yourself,
And you will be found. Amen.

7

This week we may be given
   challenges instead of ease,
      courage instead of contentment,
         opportunities instead of rest.

But we have a Savior who brings
   strength out of service,
      faith out of struggle,
         and victory out of defeat.

Go then, fearful of nothing,
   sure that in everything,
      we are held secure
         in the Master's steadfast love. Amen.

8

The Presence of God Benediction

Blessing of God be upon you;
Mercy of God abide with you;
Spirit of God direct you;
Peace of God fill you;
Through the Son of God
Who died for you. Amen.

9

Embrace the week ahead.
Be diligent in your work,
Kind to your neighbor,
Generous to the discouraged,
Patient with your family,
Loyal to the Master.

Renounce evil,
Feed the poor,
Study the Scriptures,
Begin and end the day in prayer.

In sunshine and shadow trust the Lord.
The depth of His mercy is unfathomable,
The length of His forgiveness is unmeasurable,
The flow of His love is unending.

Go rejoicing
And go in peace. Amen.

10

We are the church gathered;
Now we become the church dispersed.
May the prayers and sustenance you found here
Follow you and find you
Wherever you go.
Through Christ, who found us, called us,
And one day in His Kingdom above
Will call our names in love. Amen.

11

Followers of Christ,
Choose the will of God as your motivation,
The words of Christ as your meditation,
The promises of God as your inspiration,
The work of Christ as your salvation.

Believe this:
Christ is with you;
Christ before you;
Christ in you;
Christ over you;
Christ, your all in all. Amen.

12

Receive now
The benedictions
Of Father, Son, and Holy Spirit,
As they go before you,
Follow after you,
Guide you in the way,
And at the last
Lead you safely home. Amen.

13

Enter the world with courage.
Love God in His holiness
And all men in their need.

Espouse the faith.
Be true to yourself.
Flee temptation.
Ponder the Scriptures.

Hallow the name of God.
Rejoice in the gift of Christ.
Be directed by the Holy Spirit.

In joy or pain,
May your heart proclaim,
"Thy will be done,"
In the Master's name. Amen.

14

Love God.
Ponder Scripture.
Meditate on Christ.
Follow the Spirit.

Encourage others.
Cherish yourself.
Enjoy life.
Mediate Christian compassion.

And, when appropriate,
Don't forget to dance. Amen.

15

The Lord is with you
As you leave this place today.

Nothing will happen to you this week
That God is not aware of,
Nor that God cannot help you with
As no other.

Go then,
In the full confidence
Of God's loving presence,
And in the peace that provides
The quiet collectedness
Of the inner life.

For it is through
God the Father that we live,
In Christ Jesus we are redeemed,
By the Holy Spirit we are led and kept,
Until in heaven or on earth
We meet again.
Amen.

Bibliography

BOOKS

Aldrich, Donald B. *The Golden Book of Prayer*. New York: Dodd, Mead and Company, 1941.

Bael, Peter. *Prayer and Providence*. New York: Seabury, 1968.

Bailey, Wilfred M. *Awakened Worship*. Nashville: Abingdon Press, 1972.

Baillie, John. *A Diary of Private Prayer*. New York: Charles Scribner's Sons, 1936.

Barry, F. R., and Dearmer, P. *Westminster Prayers*. Oxford University Press, 1936.

Blackwood, Andrew W. *Leading in Public Prayer*. New York: Abingdon Press, 1958.

Bowie, Russell W. *Lift Up Your Hearts: A Collection of Prayers, Litanies, et cetera*. New York: Charles Scribner's Sons, 1936.

Brunner, Peter. *Worship in the Name of Jesus*. St. Louis: Concordia Publishing House, 1968.

Buttrick, George A. *Prayer*. Nashville: Abingdon Press, 1952.

————.*So We Believe, So We Pray*. Nashville: Abingdon Press, 1951.

————.*The Power of Prayer Today*. Waco, Tex.: Word Books, 1974.

Campbell, Ernest T. *Where Cross the Crowded Ways*. New York: Association Press, 1973.

Casteel, John. *Rediscovering Prayer*. New York: Association Press, 1955.

Christensen, James L. *Creative Ways to Worship*. Old Tappan, N.J.: Fleming H. Revell Co., 1974.

Coburn, John B. *A Life to Live—A Way to Pray*. New York: Seabury Press, 1973.

―――. *Prayer and Personal Religion*. Philadelphia: Westminster Press, 1967.

Davies, Horton. *Christian Worship: Its History and Meaning*. New York: Abingdon Press, 1957.

―――. *The Worship of the English Puritans*. Westminster: Dacre Press, 1948.

Davis, H. Grady. *Why We Worship*. Philadelphia: Muhlenberg Press, 1961.

Eddy, Robert L., ed. *Pastoral Prayers Through the Year*. New York: Charles Scribner's Sons, 1959.

Evely, Louis. *Our Prayer*. Garden City, N.Y.: Image Books, 1974.

―――. *Teach Us How To Pray*. New York: Paulist Press, 1967.

Ferguson, James, ed. *Prayers for Public Worship*. New York: Harper and Brothers, 1958.

Fisher, Fred L. *Prayer in the New Testament*. Philadelphia: Westminster Press, 1964.

Fosdick, Harry E. *A Book of Public Prayers*. New York: Harper and Brothers, 1959.

―――. *The Meaning of Prayer*. New York: Association Press, 1949.

Fox, S. F. *A Chain of Prayer Across the Ages*. John Murray, 1913.

Garrett, T. S. *Christian Worship: An Introductory Outline*. London: Oxford University Press, 1961.

Gordon, S. D. *Quiet Talks on Prayer*. New York: Grosset and Dunlap, 1941.

Glover, Carl A. *Prayers for Christian Services*. Nashville: Abingdon Press, 1959.

Hard, Larry. *Contemporary Altar Prayers*, vol. 3. Lima, Ohio: C. S. S. Publishing Co., 1973.

Hardman, Oscar. *A History of Christian Worship*. Nashville: Cokesbury Press, 1937.

Harkness, Georgia. *Prayer and the Common Life*. New York: Abingdon-Cokesbury Press, 1958.

————. *Understanding the Christian Faith*. New York: Abingdon Press, 1947.

Hoon, Paul W. *The Integrity of Worship: Pastoral Essays in Liturgical Theology*. Nashville: Abingdon Press, 1971.

Hunt, Cecil. *Uncommon Prayers*. Greenwich, Conn.: Seabury Press, 1955.

Hunter, John. *Devotional Services*. London: J. M. Dent and Sons, 1903.

Jackson, Edgar. *Understanding Prayer*. Cleveland: World Publishing Company, 1968.

Jones, James A. *Prayers for the People*. Richmond, Va.: John Knox Press, 1967.

Killinger, John. *Leave It to the Spirit*. New York: Harper and Row, 1971.

Macdonald, Alexander B. *Christian Worship in the Primitive Church*. Edinburgh: T. and T. Clark, 1934.

Macleod, Donald. *Word and Sacrament: A Preface to Preaching and Worship*. Englewood Cliffs, N.J.: Prentice-Hall, 1960.

Manschreck, Clyde L. *A History of Christianity*. Englewood Cliffs, N.J.: Prentice-Hall, 1964.

Marshall, Catherine. *The Prayers of Peter Marshall*. New York: McGraw-Hill, 1954; Lincoln, Va.: Chosen

Books, 1978.

Maxwell, William D. *An Outline of Christian Worship*. London: Oxford University Press, 1936.

———. *Concerning Worship*. London: Oxford University Press, 1949.

McCarty, Barry. *Here I Am, Lord*. Nashville: Upper Room, 1973.

Micklem, Nathaniel, ed. *Christian Worship: Studies in Its History and Meaning*. London: Oxford University Press, 1936.

Micklen, Caryl. *Contemporary Prayers for Public Worship*. Grand Rapids, Mich.: Eerdmans, 1967.

———. *More Contemporary Prayers*. Grand Rapids. Mich.: Eerdmans, 1970.

Micks, Marianne. *The Future Present*. New York: Seabury, 1970.

Noyes, Morgan Phelps, ed. *Prayers for Services*. New York: Charles Scribner's Sons, 1947.

Orchard, W. E. *The Temple*. New York: E. P. Dutton and Company, 1946.

Petry, Roy C. *A History of Christianity*. Englewood Cliffs, N.J.: Prentice-Hall, 1962.

Quoist, Michel. *Prayers*. New York: Sheed and Ward, 1963.

Rauschenbusch, Walter. *For God and the People: Prayers of the Social Awakening*. The Pilgrim Press, 1910.

Redding, David A. *If I Could Pray Again*. Westwood, N.J.: Fleming H. Revell Company, 1965.

Rottenburg, Ernest J. *Vital Elements of Public Worship*. London: Epworth Press, 1936.

Snyder, Ross. *Contemporary Celebration*. Nashville: Abingdon, 1971.

Spielmann, Richard M. *History of Christian Worship*. New York: Seabury Press, 1966.

Steere, Douglas V. *Prayer and Worship*. New York: Association Press, 1938.

The Book of Common Prayer. New York: The Church Pension Fund, 1945.

The Worshipbook. Philadelphia: Westminster Press, 1970.

Thompson, Bard. *Liturgies of the Western Church*. New York: World Publishing Company, 1961.

Trueblood, Elton. *The Lord's Prayers*. New York: Harper and Row, 1965.

Underhill, Evelyn. *Worship*. New York: Harper and Brothers, 1936.

White, James. F. *New Forms of Worship*. Nashville: Abingdon, 1971.

———. *The Worldliness of Worship*. New York: Oxford University Press, 1967.

Williams, J. Paul. *What Americans Believe and How They Worship*. Rev. ed. New York: Harper and Row, 1962.

INTERVIEWS

Brown, James Clark. First Congregational Church, San Francisco, Calif.: 15 August 1977.

Buttrick, George Arthur. 2500 Glenmary, Louisville, Ky.: 2 January 1976.

Campbell, Ernest T. The Riverside Church, New York, N.Y.: 4 March 1976.

Elson, Edward L. R., chaplain, United States Senate. Washington, D.C.: 1 March 1976.

Latch, Edward G., chaplain, United States House of Representatives. Washington, D.C.: 2 March 1976.

Read, David H. C. Madison Avenue Presbyterian Church, New York, N.Y.: 3 March 1976; Columbia Theological Seminary, Decatur, Ga.: 2 February 1978.